# EDINBURGI

## THE CITY AT A GLANC

### New Town
Comprising elegant Georgian t
cobbled streets and manicured
city's New Town is urban-planning perfection.

### Melville Monument
Architect William Burn based this 1823 tribute
to Viscount Melville, aka 'the uncrowned King
of Scotland', on Trajan's Column in Rome.
At 41m, it looms over the New Town.
*St Andrew Square*

### The Royal Scottish Academy
Reopened in 2003, the RSA hosts world-class
exhibitions. The next-door Scottish National
Gallery (T 624 6200) displays art from the
Renaissance to the late 19th century.
*The Mound, T 225 6671*

### Princes Street Gardens
Avoid the manic crush of shoppers along
Princes Street's main drag with a detour
through this pretty, peaceful park.

### Scott Monument
George Meikle Kemp's 61m monument in
honour of Sir Walter Scott was unveiled in
1846. Some see it as an example of neo-Gothic
greatness, others as a weird space rocket.
*East Princes Street Gardens*

### The Balmoral
Opened in 1902 as the North British Hotel,
this building links the architecture of the
Old Town with the neoclassicism of the New.
*1 Princes Street, T 556 2414*

### Calton Hill
Climb this magnificent incline to marvel
at the breathtaking views and the tower
celebrating Nelson's 1805 Trafalgar victory.
*See p013*

# INTRODUCTION

## THE CHANGING FACE OF THE URBAN SCENE

If looks alone were the measure of a city, the Scottish capital would rank among the world's finest. The dizzyingly romantic cobbled streets and medieval architecture of the Old Town are astonishingly intact; the Georgian splendour of the New Town's broad streets and sweeping terraces is enough to give the first-time visitor goosebumps. But don't think that this is a city trading solely on its beauty – if you get to know it, you'll discover it has a sharp, witty personality to match. Edinburgh is a centre for the arts. It has an impressive range of galleries and theatres, it boasts a respected university and a slew of bookish cafés. However, just because the city is well read, it doesn't mean it goes to bed early. Edinburgh's pubs are renowned for their relaxed licensing hours and its bars know how to mix a decent cocktail or two. And let's not forget that it still puts on Europe's biggest New Year's Eve party.

Devolution in 1999 brought a new-found confidence, and the city has been moving forward ever since. Huge sums have been spent on sprucing up the former port of Leith, renovating national art galleries and bringing trams to the centre. In fact, as far as new developments go, transport gets top billing. An airport tram link set for 2014, the refurbished Waverley Station, and, due in 2016, the Forth Replacement Crossing road bridge, will ensure that whichever route you take to Edinburgh, your first impressions will be of its bold 21st-century achievements.

# ESSENTIAL INFO

## FACTS, FIGURES AND USEFUL ADDRESSES

### TOURIST OFFICE
Edinburgh Information Centre
*3 Princes Street*
*T 473 3868*
*www.edinburgh.org*

### TRANSPORT
**Airport transfer to city centre**
Airlink buses depart regularly, 24 hours
a day. The journey takes 30 minutes
*www.flybybus.com*
**Bus**
Lothian Buses
*T 555 6363*
**Car hire**
Hertz
*10 Picardy Place*
*T 0843 309 3026*
**Taxi**
City Cabs
*T 228 1211*
There are plenty of taxi ranks and black
cabs can be safely hailed on the street
**Travel Card**
The seven-day Ridacard grants unlimited
travel on daytime bus services for £17

### EMERGENCY SERVICES
**Emergencies**
*T 999*
**Late-night pharmacy**
Boots
*46-48 Shandwick Place*
*T 225 6757*
Open until 8pm, Monday to Friday;
6pm on Saturdays; 5pm on Sundays

### CONSULATES
**US Consulate General**
*3 Regent Terrace*
*T 556 8315*
*edinburgh.usconsulate.gov*

### POSTAL SERVICES
**Post office**
*8-10 St James Centre*
*T 0845 722 3344*
**Shipping**
UPS
*T 0845 787 7877*

### BOOKS
**Exit Music** by Ian Rankin (Orion)
**Of its Time and of its Place: The Work
of Richard Murphy Architects**
by Richard MacCormac (Black Dog)
**The Prime of Miss Jean Brodie**
by Muriel Spark (Penguin Classics)

### WEBSITES
**Architecture/Design**
*www.edinburgharchitecture.co.uk*
**Art**
*www.nationalgalleries.org*
**Newspaper**
*www.scotsman.com*

### EVENTS
**Edinburgh Festival Fringe**
*www.edfringe.com*
**Edinburgh International Book Festival**
*www.edbookfest.co.uk*

### COST OF LIVING
**Taxi from Edinburgh Airport
to city centre**
£18
**Cappuccino**
£2.20
**Packet of cigarettes**
£6.50
**Daily newspaper**
£1
**Bottle of champagne**
£35

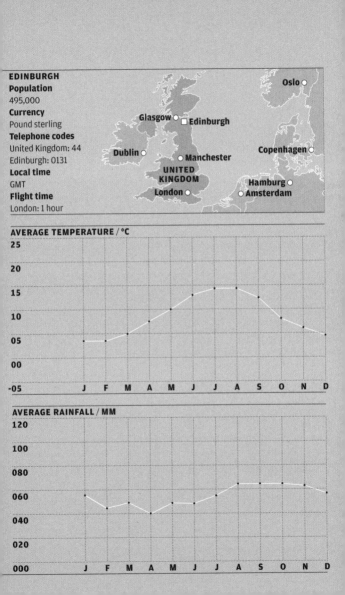

**EDINBURGH**
**Population**
495,000
**Currency**
Pound sterling
**Telephone codes**
United Kingdom: 44
Edinburgh: 0131
**Local time**
GMT
**Flight time**
London: 1 hour

Oslo
Glasgow ○ □ Edinburgh
Copenhagen ○
Dublin ○
○ Manchester
**UNITED KINGDOM**
Hamburg ○
London ○
○ Amsterdam

**AVERAGE TEMPERATURE / °C**

```
25
20
15
10
05
00
-05
    J  F  M  A  M  J  J  A  S  O  N  D
```

**AVERAGE RAINFALL / MM**

```
120
100
080
060
040
020
000
    J  F  M  A  M  J  J  A  S  O  N  D
```

# NEIGHBOURHOODS

## THE AREAS YOU NEED TO KNOW AND WHY

To help you navigate the city, we've chosen the most interesting districts (see below and the map inside the back cover) and colour-coded our featured venues, according to their location; those venues that are outside these areas are not coloured.

### LEITH

Irvine Welsh's 1993 novel, *Trainspotting*, put the city's downtrodden port on the map. Two decades on and, although some rough edges remain, Leith is transformed. Galleries, waterfront bars and cafés are booming. At the heart of the district's regeneration is food. Alongside a clutch of gastropubs, the neighbourhood can also lay claim to two Michelin-starred restaurants: Martin Wishart (54 Shore, T 553 3557) and The Kitchin (see p058).

### SOUTHSIDE/NEWINGTON

Largely residential, this is the city's least characterful zone. But it is home to the Festival Theatre (13-29 Nicholson Street, T 529 6000) and, during the Festival, the Pleasance Theatre (60 Pleasance, T 556 6550). Other draws are music venue The Queen's Hall (85-89 Clerk Street, T 668 2019), the Royal Commonwealth Pool (see p068), several university buildings and Foster + Partners' Quartermile.

### NEW TOWN

This UNESCO World Heritage Site was designed in 1767 by a young Edinburgh-born architect named James Craig. The grand Georgian terraces and their elegant neoclassical details have been meticulously maintained. Originally intended as an area purely for housing, the New Town now boasts boutique hotels, such as The Howard (see p029), and several luxury department stores (see p080).

### OLD TOWN

The city's core of medieval architecture and cobbled wynds dates back to the 12th century. Another UNESCO World Heritage Site, it is centred around the Royal Mile, which leads to the domineering Edinburgh Castle (see p010). To the south lies the Continental-style boulevard Grassmarket, lined with lively cafés and pubs. The area teems with ghost tours and tat shops, but it's impossible not to be impressed by all the historic details on show.

### WEST END/TOLLCROSS/BRUNTSFIELD

It may not be as picturesque as the Old or New Towns, but the West End does host several key arts venues, including Usher Hall (Lothian Road, T 228 1155). To the south-west, Tollcross has a somewhat seamy side to it, but emerging from this scruffy charm is Bruntsfield. Formerly a quarantine zone for plague victims, it's now a buzzy hub of boutiques, delis and handsome Victorian tenement buildings.

### CANONGATE

Essentially the lower part of the Royal Mile, this district is steeped in history and tourist attractions, including John Knox House (see p073) and the Hopkins Architects-designed 'Our Dynamic Earth' exhibition (Holyrood Road, T 550 7800). Since the arrival of the architecturally bold Scottish Parliament (see p070), opposite Holyrood Palace (T 556 5100), Canongate has become a must-visit.

# LANDMARKS
## THE SHAPE OF THE CITY SKYLINE

Climb any of Edinburgh's reputed 'Seven Hills', look down at the capital below and you'll see that the city is quite a staggering landmark in itself. The sheer lack of 20th-century development in the centre means that, on a clear day, as you survey the Gothic spires and blackened turrets towards the dramatic coastline that edges the Firth of Forth estuary, it really is a sight to behold.

In terms of city highlights, no one building shouts 'landmark' louder than Edinburgh Castle (overleaf). Built on top of a craggy escarpment as a medieval stronghold, it dominates the skyline and was the seat of Scottish royalty until the 17th century. It is the point from which the rest of Edinburgh has grown, and is a helpful navigational tool. A pinnacle of the old city, it also acts as a striking contrast to the surrounding 18th- and 19th-century architecture.

This 'newer' development encompasses the poignant and much-loved National Monument on Calton Hill (see p013), whereas more ornate buildings such as McEwan Hall (see p012), which was completed in 1897, show the extravagance that was lavished on Edinburgh's architecture during the Victorian age. Further evidence of this can be found if you take the short drive out to the Forth Rail Bridge (see p014). A masterpiece of engineering, this magnificent steel structure is as admired by locals as it is by visitors, earning it the nickname: the 'Eiffel Tower of Scotland'. *For full addresses, see Resources.*

**Edinburgh Castle**
Perched on Castle Rock, and looming
over the capital, Edinburgh Castle makes
its presence felt. It housed the Scottish
royal family until 1603, when James VI
became James I of England. Today, the
World Heritage Site is a garrison for the
British Army and has many historical
displays. A tourist magnet perhaps, but
one whose majesty surpasses most.
*Castle Hill, T 225 9846*

**McEwan Hall**

Edinburgh's students have long chuckled at the irony of graduating in a building bearing the same name as the beer that often distracted them from studying for their degrees. Irony aside, the university was fortunate that prosperous Scottish brewery owner William McEwan financed the construction of this semicircular neoclassical amphitheatre. Completed in 1897, it was the most flamboyant design of architect Sir Robert Rowand Anderson, who was also responsible for the Scottish National Portrait Gallery (see p034) on Queen Street. If you like the extravagance of the exterior, William M Palin's murals ensure the interior is just as impressive. *Bristo Square*

### National Monument

The top of Calton Hill, with its grassy slopes and panoramic views, is probably one of the first places that a local will take you to. Yet despite its popularity and central location, the peak, reached via a steep staircase climbing up the hill from Waterloo Place, is a delightfully peaceful spot to spend half an hour or so. Next to the Nelson Monument, you'll see this bizarre acropolis-style folly, designed by English architect Charles Robert Cockerell and Scotsman William Playfair. Modelled on the Parthenon in Athens and dedicated to those who perished in the Napoleonic Wars, its construction began in 1824 but it was never fully completed. At the time, this was seen as a national scandal. Today, however, it only adds to the lyrical feel of this characterful hilltop.

*Calton Hill*

### Forth Rail Bridge

It is perhaps indicative of Edinburgh's good fortune that although it was hardly touched by the Industrial Revolution (the city remained essentially professional), it still benefited from the most expensive, most beautiful feat of Victorian British engineering. The Forth Rail Bridge was designed by Sir Benjamin Baker and Sir John Fowler and completed in 1890. The cantilevered steel structure rises imperiously from the Firth of Forth, and stretches 2.5km across the estuary to Fife. Despite the popular myth that repainting the bridge is an endless task, the job was completed, ahead of schedule, in 2011. Trainspotting in Edinburgh may have taken on a new meaning thanks to Irvine Welsh, but as far as the hobby goes, there's no better place to do it than here.
*Queensferry*

# HOTELS

## WHERE TO STAY AND WHICH ROOMS TO BOOK

For such a small city, Edinburgh attracts a huge number of visitors. At Hogmanay and during the Festival, there's no room at the inn, but booking well ahead is advisable over the rest of the summer as well. The grand Georgian residences in the New Town make perfect boutique hotels, but with only a handful of rooms in each, they fill up quickly. For this kind of intimate accommodation, The Howard (see p029) is a good option, whereas others, such as One Royal Circus (see p028), offer posh B&B-style service. Or stay at an actual B&B, in the chic, albeit out-of-the-way 94DR (see p020). If five-star facilities and a central location top your priorities, two luxuriously reworked railway hotels stand sentinel at either end of Princes Street: Rocco Forte's The Balmoral (No 1, T 556 2414), and The Caledonian (see p024), revamped in 2012. Other additions include The Atholl (see p018), an opulent four-suite hideaway, and, at the other end of the spectrum, the first UK property from design-savvy German chain Motel One (18-21 Market Street, T 220 0730). Looking forward, Gareth Hoskins Architects' redevelopment of the Royal High School into a hotel is one to watch out for.

If you crave more contemporary surroundings, The Glasshouse (2 Greenside Place, T 525 8200), which has large rooms and lots of outside space, provides a modern take on the traditional Scottish interior, whereas Tigerlily (see p030) is best for party animals. *For full addresses and room rates, see Resources.*

### The Witchery

If you're looking for eccentricity, opt for one of the nine theatrical suites located at the top of a winding stone staircase above James Thomson's celebrated restaurant of the same name, and across the street in a second historic building. This is Gothic glamour at its most extreme, each room boasting antiques and curiosities, roll-top baths for two people and complimentary champagne; many also have four-posters draped in velvet. Forget wi-fi, plasma screens and power showers, The Witchery is all about romance. Think Versace does Victoriana and you're some of the way to envisaging the lust den that is the Old Rectory. Alternatively check into the Heriot Suite for its chapel bathroom (above) and panoramic views across the Old Town. *Castlehill, The Royal Mile, T 225 5613, www.thewitchery.com*

### The Atholl

Atholl Crescent has long been associated with gastronomic expertise. In 1891, the Edinburgh College of Domestic Science moved in, occupying 12 of the elegant Georgian townhouses by the 1960s. After a stint as the offices of a law firm, No 11 is now a culinary hotspot once again. Opened as a four-suite hotel in 2012, The Atholl's main draw is its in-room dining, overseen by Albert Roux; each accommodation comes with a private chef. Less hotel, more luxury serviced apartment, The Atholl's interiors are by Ian Smith Design, who kept the original Georgian features, including a dramatic cupola and ornate cornicing. Book The Abercromby suite (opposite and above) for an indulgent break – it has a hot tub and private terrace. *11 Atholl Crescent, T 08447 360 047, www.theatholl.com*

## 94DR

One of the best features of this 21st-century B&B is also the worst – its location. On a busy road in Southside, a 10-minute ride from the centre, what 94DR lacks in convenience it makes up for in the sense of calm you get from staying at arm's length from the hordes. Amid the torrent of tartan that rampages through the city's guesthouses, Paul Lightfoot and John MacEwan's elegant townhouse has style. Flowers brighten its tiled entrance hall, cooked-to-order breakfasts are seasonal, there is an honesty bar, and attention to detail is such that showers have taps set to one side so you don't get a wet arm when you switch them on. The Bowmore (pictured) is our room key of choice.
*94 Dalkeith Road, T 662 9265, www.94dr.com*

### Hotel Missoni

Although you won't find many clues to its presence (unless you count the doormen's Missoni-print kilts), slip between two colossal ceramic vases into the world's first Missoni hotel and you'll be met by a genuine buzz. The bar (opposite) is the closest Edinburgh gets to Miami, manned by staff with model good looks who serve a sharp line in cocktails. Upstairs is Cucina, a modern Italian restaurant developed in collaboration with Giorgio Locatelli. A small spa offers Eve Lom and Natura Bissé treatments. Against a bold backdrop, which is heavy on the brand's trademark multicolour zigzags, the Missoni caters for tech-loving guests, offering free in-room wi-fi, iPod docks and Nespresso machines. Best beds in the house? Room 507, with its killer view of the castle, or the luxe penthouse Suite D'Argento (above).
*1 George IV Bridge, T 220 6666,*
*www.hotelmissoni.com*

## The Caledonian

For years, 'The Caley' was a faded fixture on Princes Street. That changed in 2012 when this Victorian railway hotel, first opened in 1903, became a Waldorf Astoria and underwent a £24m facelift. Rooms were revamped by D + Company, and Fox Linton Associates led the renewal of the public spaces, creating the chandelier-clad, marble-floored interior, which is now as grand as the building's stately sandstone facade. Of the 241 rooms and suites, ask for a castle view from one with wood-panelled walls and richly textured furnishings, rather than a room in the 1970s wing out the back. French haute cuisine is served at the Galvin brothers' Pompadour by Galvin (T 222 8975). *Princes Street, T 222 8890, www.thecaledonianedinburgh.com*

**Prestonfield**

This distinctive 17th-century mansion on the edge of Holyrood Park, 15 minutes by cab from the centre, was home to the Dick-Cunyngham family for 300 years. A hotel for five decades, it has hosted guests such as Oliver Reed and Joan Collins. In 2004, it was bought by local restaurateur and hotelier James Thomson of The Witchery (see p017), who turned it into something of a lavish folly. Many of the 23 rooms and suites, including the splendid Allan Ramsay Suite (above), are decked out with sleigh beds, velvet drapes and indecent amounts of silk. If you're a minimalist, stay away, but for a decadent weekend, Prestonfield is hard to beat. Enjoy a meal in the opulent Rhubarb Restaurant (opposite, T 225 1333), before retiring to the candlelit Tapestry Room for a postprandial dram beneath the ancestral portraits.
*Priestfield Road, T 225 7800,*
*www.prestonfield.com*

### One Royal Circus

Husband-and-wife team Mike and Susan Gordon moved into this elegant townhouse in 1998. Ten years and two children later, they concluded that it was better suited to entertaining guests, so they now run it as a B&B. The five well-designed rooms and suites are simple but luxurious: beds are dressed with Frette cotton sheets and goosedown duvets, and each en suite boasts top-to-toe limestone tiling and top-of-the-range fittings. But it is the rest of the house that really sets this residence apart from any other hotel in the city. At your disposal are a bar, a large kitchen, a sitting room, a games room and a gym, not to mention the striking main hall (above) and staircase. Best of all, there's no sign outside to announce this is a hotel.
*1 Royal Circus, T 625 6669,*
*www.oneroyalcircus.com*

## The Howard

Staying here comes a competitive second to actually living in one of the Georgian apartments that line the avenues of the New Town. Set on one of the area's most impressive roads, The Howard comprises three sophisticated townhouses. Eighteen rooms, each named after a local street, are splendidly decked out but with plenty of home comforts, as in the Abercromby Suite (above). Every effort is made to forge a 'non-hotel' atmosphere: you get a key rather than a card, there's no booming air conditioning, the windows actually open and you're not bombarded by branding. Coupled with personal touches, such as your own butler and a cup of tea with your wake-up call, this attention to detail makes The Howard a model boutique hotel.
*34 Great King Street, T 557 3500, www.thehoward.com*

### Tigerlily

This rock'n'roll hotel makes no attempt at self-restraint, much like its cocktail bar and club, Lulu, in the basement. But the 33 rooms are more than just a place to lay your head after one too many, and are, in fact, very chic. For pure decadence, reserve one of the two Georgian Suites (pictured). *125 George Street, T 225 5005, www.tigerlilyedinburgh.co.uk*

# 24 HOURS

## SEE THE BEST OF THE CITY IN JUST ONE DAY

If you take just one piece of advice when in Edinburgh, it should be to wear comfortable shoes. Although there's no shortage of taxis around for late nights and the inevitable cloudbursts, if you don't put in the legwork you'll miss out on what makes this capital so impressive. Short cuts through its cobbled streets and hidden closes will reveal tucked-away art galleries, unassuming eateries and inconspicuous shops selling beguiling wares. Alternatively, it could be the promenade along the newly developed docks at Leith or the sharp climb up Arthur's Seat or Calton Hill to admire one of the many breathtaking views that will lodge in your mind.

Luckily, Edinburgh is wonderfully compact and there are plenty of excellent places to fuel up as you plot your route. Start with a great Scottish breakfast or some delicious eggs at Urban Angel (opposite), after which you'll be ready to tackle the city's resurgent art scene at the renovated Scottish National Portrait Gallery (see p034). For lunch, stroll round the corner to The Dogs (see p036), a local favourite serving hearty fare that has a retro flavour. A short walk past North Bridge brings you to the imaginative installations of the Ingleby Gallery (see p038). Come nightfall, strike out to The Gardener's Cottage (see p039), where two of the city's brightest stars weave their culinary magic, before heading on to the gin bar at Stac Polly (29-33 Dublin Street, T 556 2231), launched in 2013. *For full addresses, see Resources.*

### 10.00 Urban Angel

For laidback brunch or a brisk breakfast, this basement café is a firm favourite; in fact, crowds gather outside on weekends, tempted by the French toast. Here, as in a sister outpost in Forth Street (T 556 6323), owner Gilly MacPherson has hit on a simple formula – a sleek but cosy venue serving top-notch food at a decent price. Order a free-range eggs Benedict with smoked haddock, or porridge with heather honey, and feel smug about your responsible consumerism – almost all the ingredients are Fairtrade, organic or locally sourced, and there's a line of products, from jams and chutneys to organic wine, available to buy. Featuring a polished flagstone floor and simple contemporary wooden furniture, the decor is also spot-on. *121 Hanover Street, T 225 6215, www.urban-angel.co.uk*

### 11.30 Scottish National Portrait Gallery

Reinvigorated in 2011 by Glasgow's Page\ Park firm after a three-year, £17.6m refurb, the SNPG is now closer to architect Sir Robert Rowand Anderson's original 1889 designs than it was for much of the 20th century. Visitors can access three floors and a larger showcase of its portrait and photography collections in new spaces such as the Contemporary Gallery. An increase in natural light has been made possible by the removal of partition walls and suspended ceilings. Highlights include Alexander Nasmyth's painting of Robert Burns, and Robert Adamson and David Octavius Hill's 19th-century photograph of a Newhaven fishwife. The magnificent suite of galleries on the top floor (Gallery Five, above) should not be missed.
*1 Queen Street, T 624 6200,*
*www.nationalgalleries.org*

### 14.00 The Dogs

David Ramsden's shabby chic gastropub is a perennial Edinburgh favourite. He may have downsized in 2012, when his basement bar Underdogs closed its doors, but Ramsden's restaurant was always the main draw, serving great modern Scottish food in a first-floor Georgian apartment. Such unaffected dining is hard to find in the city.
*110 Hanover Street, T 220 1208*

### 16.00 Ingleby Gallery

Britain's largest private contemporary art gallery outside London, the Ingleby was founded in 1998. Despite now being one of the grandes dames of the Edinburgh art scene, it still has a freshness about it, partly due to a move to a larger site in 2008. Since setting up shop in a former nightclub behind Waverley Station, owners Florence and Richard Ingleby have created a space suited to the tranquil appreciation of artists such as Peter Liversidge, Alison Watt, James Hugonin, Howard Hodgkin and the late Ian Hamilton Finlay, as well as collaborative installations like *Gravity's Rainbow* (above). Don't miss the gallery's quarterly Billboard for Edinburgh project, which utilises the building's hoarding to showcase public artwork.
*15 Calton Road, T 556 4441, www.inglebygallery.com*

**20.00** The Gardener's Cottage

A once dilapidated, listed 19th-century cottage now provides the setting for a taste of the country in the heart of the city. Edinburgh's seasonal and sustainable revolution continues to gain momentum here with chefs Edward Murray and Dale Mailley leading the way, their CVs loaded with stints in the capital's top restaurants, as well as their own temporary pop-up at Edinburgh Farmers' Market. The interiors were done on a budget and the end result is a pleasingly rustic spot with communal wooden tables, salvaged chairs and mismatched china. The garden provides herbs and vegetables, which feature on a daily changing menu that includes dishes such as hake with mash, wild leeks and broccoli. Closed Tuesdays and Wednesdays. *1 Royal Terrace Gardens, T 558 1221, www.thegardenerscottage.co*

# URBAN LIFE
## CAFÉS, RESTAURANTS, BARS AND NIGHTCLUBS

Edinburgh's culinary scene has transformed over the past decade and the city has been steadily gaining a reputation as one of the best in the UK for eating out. Five of its chefs – Paul Kitching (see p050), Tom Kitchin (see p058), Jeff Bland at The Balmoral's in-house restaurant Number One (1 Princes Street, T 557 6727), Martin Wishart (see p059) and Dominic Jack of Castle Terrace (33-35 Castle Terrace, T 229 1222) – hold a Michelin star.

As the headline acts have won plaudits, a fine supporting cast has stepped up to the plate. French-inspired brasserie The Honours (see p059) is invariably fully booked, as is Mark Greenaway's restaurant (opposite). In the Old Town, Andrew and Lisa Radford's Timberyard (see p048) is making waves, and Tom Kitchin and Dominic Jack have teamed up again to open gastropub The Scran & Scallie (1 Comely Bank Road). Meanwhile, authentic French spots, such as L'Escargot Bleu (56 Broughton Street, T 557 1600) and La Garrigue (31 Jeffrey Street, T 557 3032), continue to thrive.

Although you're never far from liquid refreshment here, you'll need to choose your pubs carefully. Most are welcoming, but some can be sniffy to non-locals and others have lost their charm. Bars are less risky: Bramble (see p044) is the drinking den du jour and The Voodoo Rooms (19a West Register Street, T 556 7060) draws a clued-up crowd to its live music and glam surroundings.
*For full addresses, see Resources.*

### Restaurant Mark Greenaway

One of 2013's most anticipated openings was the relocation of Mark Greenaway's progressive British restaurant to the New Town from Picardy Place. The new space, in a renovated Georgian townhouse where the interior design is by Adam Storey (see p062), combines eye-catching clusters of Victorian brass chandeliers with teal walls and large mirrors overlaid with maps of the city. This is the place to satiate a sweet tooth – try the broken citrus tart with yuzu parfait, frozen shortbread and pistachio purée – but the starters and mains are none too shabby either. The building was once a bank and the wine cellar is housed below in the old vaults: tip the sommelier Loic Druyver a wink and he'll take you down to sample the wines.
*69 North Castle Street, T 226 1155, www.markgreenaway.com*

## Earthy

The Earthy story began in 2008 in an old Southside printworks when a foodie, a farmer and a horticulturalist got together and hatched a plan to turn it into a 'food hub'. The resulting café and deli, where staff are known as Earthlings, offers wholesome food. Dishes such as organic sweet potato, ginger and coconut milk soup are served alongside products from 200 Scottish producers, which help to bridge the gap between the city's weekly farmers' markets. The homespun ethos also extends to the design, which includes recycled timber salvaged from skips, and seating made by local craftsmen from wind-damaged trees. A walled market garden opened in 2013. The Earthy empire encompasses two other outlets: a shop in Portobello (T 344 7930) and a restaurant and food store in Canonmills (T 556 9696). *33-41 Ratcliffe Terrace, T 667 2967, www.earthy.uk.com*

## Bramble

With just a touch of the speakeasy about it, Bramble is easily one of the city's top bars. Its smoke-and-mirrors interior, so compact that you assume there must be another hidden room (there isn't), attracts a mixed crowd of regulars and in-the-know out-of-towners. Pile into this underground drinking den late in the evening to recline on worn leather armchairs or sprawl into cosy, cushion-strewn alcoves in flickering candlelight, while the DJ does his thing and bartenders mix the best cocktails in town; try the signature Bramble and you will see what we mean. Down the hill in Stockbridge, owners Mike Aikman and Jason Scott have opened a second bar, The Last Word (T 225 9009), in the space of their former restaurant The Saint. *16a Queen Street, T 226 6343, www.bramblebar.co.uk*

### Kay's Bar

Tucked away in what looks as if it's a period cottage in the heart of the New Town, Kay's is an authentic Victorian pub dolled out in red velvet. Regulars, mostly men of a certain age, have earned their places around the bar, where you will find the handlebar-moustached barman and manager Fraser Gillespie dispensing local ales and a selection of about 50 malts. Friendly and welcoming, the pub serves a top-notch lunch of haggis, neeps (swede) and tatties, but really comes into its own on quiet winter evenings, when the fire's roaring and you can play a game of Scrabble in the wood-panelled library. *39 Jamaica Street, T 225 1858, www.kaysbar.co.uk*

### Kanpai

The name means 'bottoms up' in Japanese, but this stylish sushi joint is more of a place to sip sake than to down a few. The interiors, devised by Leith-based agency Four-by-Two (see p062), are inspired by contemporary Tokyo sushi bars, with rhythmic slatted oak panels throughout. The space is divided into three areas: the modern bar clad in rough-cut, solid timber blocks where you can watch the Japanese-trained chefs at work; a private dining area (opposite); and the minimal dining room itself (above), which has textured wallpaper cast with Japanese prints. As well as sushi, the menu includes grilled dishes and teppanyaki, and there's a small but well-selected sake list: we suggest the full-bodied and dry Kasumi Tsuru.
*8-10 Grindlay Street, T 228 1602,*
*www.kanpaisushi.co.uk*

### Timberyard

You can't (and shouldn't) miss Andrew and Lisa Radford's 2012 venture, which announces itself via an industrial-scale red doorway near the College of Art. Timberyard is split into multiple areas, each with a nod to the space's previous incarnation (the clue is in the name). This includes the Shed, a brick outhouse for private dining that has a cosy wood-burner, and the Warehouse (pictured), where bare light bulbs hang from a high ceiling. The Radfords' son, Ben, heads up the kitchen, producing artful dishes like beech-smoked sirloin with ramson and January king cabbage. Younger brother Jo leads the bar, serving up the sort of warm spiced cider that'll make you grateful for the city's bleak climes. *10 Lady Lawson Street, T 221 1222, www.timberyard.co*

## 21212

Once you've got your head around the name (it refers to the menu — a choice of two dishes, then a single set dish, followed by a choice of two more dishes; you get the idea), turn your attention to the decor. Royal Terrace is one of the city's Georgian jewels, and 21212 has taken the opulence and run with it. As OTT as Louis XIV, it features expensively papered walls and ripplingly luxurious banquettes. And the food? Handing over responsibility to chef-owner Paul Kitching is liberating. Dishes may read as if they're crazed shopping lists — creamy gruyère risotto with six types of mushroom, cucumber wafers, smoked duck, pak choi and a white truffle-oil sauce— but the reward is one of the most entertaining meals in town. *3 Royal Terrace, T 523 1030, www.21212restaurant.co.uk*

## Bia Bistrot

There's nothing like bagging a table in a popular neighbourhood restaurant to make you feel as though you've found a direct short cut to the heart of the city, and Bia Bistrot, in Edinburgh's wealthy Morningside area, is exactly that. A find for visiting foodies, and with a host of regular punters, it punches above its weight via inventive but relaxed cooking at reasonable prices. Bia means 'food'

in Irish Gaelic, and the ethos here is one of openness and conviviality, aimed at providing a laidback atmosphere. That's partly achieved through dedication to quality local ingredients, and fish are supplied by Campbells in Linlithgow, dairy from Bonaly Farm in Loanhead and cheeses by IJ Mellis (see p080). *19 Colinton Road, T 452 8453, www.biabistrot.co.uk*

## Peter's Yard

Foster + Partners' redevelopment of the former Royal Infirmary (now known as Quartermile) may be uninspiring, but one of its redeeming features is this café/bakery. The pale, clean-lined interiors by Norrgavel provide a refreshing change from the boho coffee bars that litter the city. Founded by Swedish master baker Jan Hedh, Peter's Yard entices customers through its glass doors with a pile of rustic artisan breads on the counter. Inside, the café offers Scandinavian-style treats, a superb lunch menu, homemade conserves, mouth-watering cakes and desserts, gourmet chocolate and the best coffee in town. A second branch opened in 2012 in Stockbridge (T 332 2901), where the signature sourdough pizzas are a hit.

*Quartermile, 27 Simpson Loan,*
*T 228 5876, www.petersyard.com*

### Sheep Heid Inn

The schlep up Arthur's Seat from Holyrood Park, and the scramble down the other side to sup a pint in Scotland's oldest pub, is a popular weekend jaunt for locals. The Sheep Heid Inn dates to 1360, and is said to have got its name after King James VI presented the landlord with an ornate ram's head snuff box in 1580 after a game of skittles in the yard. The original skittle alley is still here, but the ancient hostelry was acquired by the Mitchells & Butlers group in 2011. The takeover, and ensuing restoration, has split regulars; some think the refit has smartened it up whereas others claim the drinking den has been turned into a homogenised gastropub. Decide for yourself over a Sunday roast, washed down with a cask ale amid the roaring fire, rustic floorboards and mounted rams' heads.
*43-45 The Causeway, T 661 7974, www.thesheepheidedinburgh.co.uk*

## Ondine

Since this pescatarian dream ticket opened in 2009, no seafood lover has been able to set foot in the Scottish capital without a visit to Ondine. Headed by Edinburgh-born chef Roy Brett, who has worked with Rick Stein, the restaurant goes beyond the traditional Scottish 'fish supper' (that's fish and chips to the rest of us) to serve the most sophisticated fish and shellfish in the city. Take a pew at the horseshoe-shaped crustacean bar and feast on fresh oysters, lobster, clams and langoustines. Or book a table and tuck into grilled lemon sole, sea bream curry or, if you must have your food deep-fried, tempura squid with Vietnamese dipping sauce. Every sliver of seafood served is accredited by the Marine Stewardship Council (MSC).

*2 George IV Bridge, T 226 1888,*
*www.ondinerestaurant.co.uk*

**The Shore Bar & Restaurant**

One of the country's first gastropubs, The Shore opened its doors more than 30 years ago and has matured into a much-loved fixture on Leith's waterfront, its lively bar and cosy dining room unchanging from year to year. Now owned by a local restaurant group, the kitchen's focus is on seafood, as well as pub classics such as rump of lamb and, for dessert, a moreish treacle tart. Full menus are available from noon until 10pm seven days a week, and an unhurried, easygoing atmosphere persists. Befitting The Shore's casual appeal, there are plenty of wines available by the glass. *3 Shore, T 553 5080, www.fishersbistros.co.uk*

### The Kitchin

Proprietor and head chef Tom Kitchin draws a serious crowd to his waterfront restaurant, located in a uniform row of eateries and bars in Leith's Commercial Quay. The Kitchin caused a flurry of excitement when it opened in 2006, and a Michelin star awarded just seven months later confirmed that the hype was justified. The cuisine features mainly seasonal Scottish produce, prepared using French techniques. Despite the elegant interior, the place has never quite taken off as the glam haunt it was perhaps intended to be, but its relaxed, friendly vibe makes fine dining an unintimidating experience.
*78 Commercial Quay, T 555 1755, www.thekitchin.com*

### The Honours

For more than a decade, Martin Wishart's eponymous Leith restaurant (T 553 3557) has enchanted foodies from Edinburgh and beyond. In July 2011, the Michelin-starred chef's acolytes gained a new place of worship, when The Honours opened just off Queen Street. The brasserie, led by right-hand man Paul Tamburrini, draws punchy flavours from Scottish produce, resulting in dishes such as crispy pork belly on spiced lentils with sea scallops and apple. The three-course lunch prix-fixe menu is fairly priced at £17.50. Long-standing collaborators Ian Smith Design created the interiors, and rather than emulate Wishart's subdued fine-dining sister restaurant, Smith got out his set square for a bold, geometric look.
*58a North Castle Street, T 220 2513, www.thehonours.co.uk*

### Sweet Melindas

There's an intimacy and a knowing buzz here that you won't find in any other Southside restaurant. Tucked away in the residential quarter of Marchmont, Sweet Melindas is a tiny fish restaurant, with a charming decor of white panelled walls and black-and-white photos. Owner and chef Kevin O'Connor is serious about making everything from scratch, from the soda bread to the chocolate truffles.

The short menu changes daily, serving sustainable fish bought at Eddie's Seafood Market next door, such as the home-cured dill and gin gravlax with dill mayonnaise and cucumber salad. A reasonably priced wine list and some devilishly good desserts help to ensure a loyal clientele. Sweet Melindas closes on Sundays and Mondays.
*11 Roseneath Street, T 229 7953,*
*www.sweetmelindas.co.uk*

# INSIDERS' GUIDE

**FEE AND ADAM STOREY, DESIGNERS**

The owners of concept boutique Life Story (see p084), Fee and Adam Storey live in Leith, where they enjoy views of Arthur's Seat. Fee, born and bred in Edinburgh, is a textile designer; her husband Adam is creative director of the design agency Four-by-Two. 'We choose to live here because there's a real mix of people: photographers, architects, filmmakers and designers,' says Fee.

Since opening their shop off Broughton Street, the pair have become regulars of nearby café and roastery Artisan Roast (No 57, T 07526 236 615), and Crombies (No 97-101, T 557 0111), which, Fee says, 'has the best sausages in town'. During the week, Adam takes clients to Printworks Coffee (42 Constitution Street, T 555 7070) or, if 'something a little stronger is required', for a drink at Monteiths (61 High Street, T 557 0330). At the end of the day, Fee often pays a visit to the Whitespace gallery (11 Gayfield Square, T 07814 514 771). 'I like that it offers drop-in drawing classes,' she says. Weekends are sometimes filled with bicycle rides along the Water of Leith, or perhaps by shopping for menswear at Dick's (3 North West Circus Place, T 226 6220) or jewellery at Hannah Zakari (43 Candlemaker Row, T 516 3264). Adam likes to surf; Tyninghame Beach in East Lothian is a favoured destination. 'We head out armed with a flask of coffee, and a book and a blanket so that Fee can chill out on the shore,' he says.

*For full addresses, see Resources.*

# ARCHITOUR

## A GUIDE TO EDINBURGH'S ICONIC BUILDINGS

The fact that Edinburgh is blessed with some of the finest historic buildings in the country makes it ideal for architourists, but it is a huge burden on working architects based here. Until 20 years ago, there was essentially a moratorium on changing the landscape in the centre, which was in some danger of turning into a museum rather than the buzzing heart of a modern capital. However, the 1990s brought a need for office space and housing, and an easing of the draconian planning laws. It was acknowledged that the new could be successfully blended with the old, and the Scottish Storytelling Centre (see p073), Dovecot Studios' tapestry centre (see p076) and, set for 2014, the £130m spruce up of Waverley Station – with a roof made from 24,700 glazed panels – have been praised for stitching threads of modernity into the existing fabric.

Indeed, Edinburgh has grown so confident about contemporary architecture that it now boasts one of Britain's most innovative structures. The 2004 Scottish Parliament (see p070), created by the late Enric Miralles, became a turning point for the city's built environment. Those who love it say it is a building to be proud of, one which opened up the architectural arena for a freer approach. Others regard the enterprise as a disaster – three years late and, at a total cost of £414m, hugely over budget, matched only by the problematic, runaway tram project that upturned Princes Street. *For full addresses, see Resources.*

### National Museum of Scotland

Hot on the heels of the refurbishment of the Scottish National Portrait Gallery (see p034) came a major overhaul of the Victorian section of the National Museum of Scotland (formerly the Royal Museum). The £47m undertaking, completed in 2011, resulted in the oldest part of the country's flagship museum (above) being restored to its glass-ceilinged glory by Balfour Beatty and specialists Beck Interiors. Thanks to the redevelopment, there's no longer an odd partnership between the slightly careworn relic and the bold architectural extension attached to it in 1998 by Benson & Forsyth (overleaf). Now both buildings combine to offer more public space, an interactive technology zone, updated displays and a new café and shop. *Chambers Street, T 0300 123 6789, www.nms.ac.uk*

### Royal Commonwealth Pool

Most locals tend to ignore this brutalist building and head straight to the Olympic-size swimming pool inside. We'd advise you to linger and admire the view before taking your dip. Designed by Robert Matthew, a protégé of the great Scottish architect Basil Spence, the Category-A-listed complex was constructed as one of the venues for the 1970 Commonwealth Games, and has been popular with the public ever since. The 'Commie', as it's known, reopened in spring 2012 after a £37m refurbishment that lasted nearly three years, and continues to serve as a top-level training facility for the country's Olympic-standard swimmers. A new 25m pool with a moveable floor will host the diving competition of the 2014 Commonwealth Games.
*21 Dalkeith Road, T 667 7211,*
*www.edinburghleisure.co.uk*

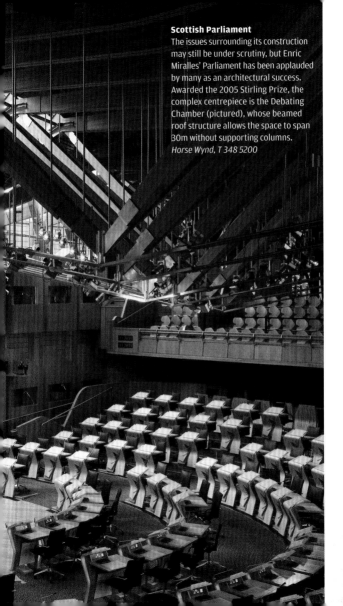

**Scottish Parliament**
The issues surrounding its construction
may still be under scrutiny, but Enric
Miralles' Parliament has been applauded
by many as an architectural success.
Awarded the 2005 Stirling Prize, the
complex centrepiece is the Debating
Chamber (pictured), whose beamed
roof structure allows the space to span
30m without supporting columns.
*Horse Wynd, T 348 5200*

## Old College

The home of Edinburgh University's School of Law took more than half a century (1789 to 1840) to finish. The brothers of original architect Robert Adam – James and William – were followed by William Playfair in supervising the build after his death, and Sir Robert Rowand Anderson added the dome in 1887. A dramatic stone arch announces the entrance to Old College, and although its attractive courtyard was being used as a car park until 2010, even that couldn't take away from the impact of Adam's landmark. In 2011, a grassed quadrangle proposed by Playfair in his original design, which was never realised due to lack of funds, finally came to fruition through a plan from local firm Simpson & Brown. It is sympathetic to the architect's original vision.

*South Bridge, www.law.ed.ac.uk/tour*

### Scottish Storytelling Centre

In one of Britain's most protected urban zones, the Netherbow, perched on the Royal Mile and adjacent to the listed John Knox House, which dates to 1470, Malcolm Fraser Architects masterfully set the modern next to the ancient. The Scottish Storytelling Centre is a scheme that aims to revive a dying oral tradition. Take a peek inside to witness how the light, informal interior spaces of the 21st-century building juxtapose effortlessly with the 15th-century house next door. The contemporary bell tower displays a plaque, once mounted above the archway of the old Netherbow gate to the city, and over which the heads of executed criminals were impaled. It also features the Netherbow Bell, which tolled as prisoners were led to their deaths. *43-45 High Street, T 556 9579, www.scottishstorytellingcentre.co.uk*

### Randolph Crescent

Drawing from experience gained on previous Georgian New Town projects Moray Place and Ainslie Place, the Earl of Moray and architect James Gillespie Graham created a softer, less uniform structure for Randolph Crescent, built between 1822 and 1855. With fewer straight lines and a less austere feel, it's little wonder that it is a frequently used backdrop for period dramas.

### Dovecot Studios

This highly regarded but little-known gallery blends the city's past and present to great effect. The space was previously a swimming pool, in use from 1885 until the 1990s, when dereliction meant the first public baths in Edinburgh had to be closed. To the rescue flew Dovecot Studios, a world-class contemporary tapestry firm, which celebrated its centenary in 2012. Dovecot moved in after a reinvention of the space in 2009, and tapestry-weaving is integral to the project. The company also works with artists, curators and arts organisations to provide exhibitions and events that explore craft in the 21st century. In 2011, the Dovecot Café by Stag Espresso (T 07590 728 974), specialising in locally sourced produce, opened on site.
*10 Infirmary Street, T 550 3660,*
*www.dovecotstudios.com*

### Royal Botanic Garden

A perennial favourite of visitors to the city, what was founded in the 1600s as a physic garden now extends over 28 hectares of painstakingly landscaped grounds just north of the town centre. An imaginative exhibition and events programme engages with Edinburgh's communities to keep the public, as well as horticulture buffs, returning. In 2009, the opening of a visitor centre at the garden's sedum-roofed John Hope Gateway (pictured), reinvigorated the whole experience. Named after John Hope, the Garden's royal keeper from 1761 to 1786, this award-winning low-carbon building by Edward Cullinan Architects incorporates a restaurant, a shop, a nursery and a gallery. *Arboretum Place, T 552 7171, www.rbge.org.uk*

# SHOPPING

## THE BEST RETAIL THERAPY AND WHAT TO BUY

Princes Street and George Street vie for the title of Edinburgh's main shopping drag. Between the two stands Jenners (48 Princes Street, T 225 2442), Scotland's stateliest department store. Nearby, Harvey Nichols (30-34 St Andrew Square, T 524 8388), Louis Vuitton (1-2 Multrees Walk North, T 652 5900) and Emporio Armani (25 Multrees Walk, T 523 1580) keep label-lovers satisfied.

For specialist boutiques, the steep and winding cobbled Victoria Street is home to several gems, including IJ Mellis Cheesemonger (No 30a, T 226 6215), art bookshop Analogue (see p085) and tailor Walker Slater (see p082). Vintage fans should visit Armstrongs (83 Grassmarket, T 220 5557) and Godiva Boutique (9 West Port, T 221 9212). You'll find covetable furniture at Tangram Furnishers (33-37 Jeffrey Street, T 556 6551) and Catalog Ltd (2-4 St Stephen Place, T 225 2888), home accessories at Moleta Munro (4 Jeffrey Street, T 557 4800), and one-off gifts at Life Story (see p084) and Concrete Wardrobe (50a Broughton Street, T 558 7130).

If you're on the hunt for edible treats, the Saturday farmers' market (9am to 2pm) on Castle Terrace is a must, as is a trip to German baker Falko Konditormeister (185 Bruntsfield Place, T 656 0763). Another essential is Italian deli Valvona & Crolla (19 Elm Row, T 556 6066), which also owns VinCaffè (11 Multrees Walk, T 557 0088), ideally located for a post-shopping coffee stop.

*For full addresses, see Resources.*

**Bruichladdich Scotch Whisky**

One of the most exciting independent craft distillers in Scotland, Bruichladdich dates from 1881, but business declined until a rescue party led by Mark Reynier arrived in 2000. The whisky has since become known for its limited bottlings and purity; it's neither coloured nor chill-filtered. And the forward-looking product design helps single-malt shed its whiskery image. Islay's only organic single-malt,

The Organic 2010 (above), £38, is, in the words of Bruichladdich's master distiller, Jim McEwan, 'an elegant, composed and stylish young spirit'. Taste it in Edinburgh at the Whiski Rooms (T 225 7224), which is an unfussy venue that stocks about 300 whiskies; these are also available to buy in the specialist in-house shop.
*Isle of Islay, T 01496 850 190*
*www.bruichladdich.com*

**Walker Slater**
If the thought of garish tartan and scratchy wool has put you off Scottish tailoring, your faith will be restored here. Walker Slater stocks its own collection of wool jumpers, cords, tweed jackets and bespoke suits, as well as select British brands such as Albert Thurston. In 2012, a womenswear outlet opened down the street at No 46 (T 225 4257). *20 Victoria Street. T 220 2636*

### Life Story

This lifestyle concept store, opened in 2012, is the brainchild of husband-and-wife team Fee and Adam Storey (see p062), and brings a new kind of retail experience to design-savvy shoppers in the capital. Fashion and homewares accessories are sourced from around the globe, including knitwear from Orkney-based Hilary Grant, washi tape from Japan, and assorted taxidermy. The story of each product is displayed on a swing tag or recounted by Fee to curious customers. The honey-hued interior is also home to a showpiece back wall created from a kilometre of wooden planks, which acts as both a sculptural hanging area with flexible rails and shelves, and a screen separating the store from Fee's studio and design business, Alphabet. *53 London Street, T 629 9699, www.lifestoryshop.com*

### Analogue

It's not just because it stocks Wallpaper*
City Guides among its set of design, art
and architecture titles that we've included
Analogue here. Originally opened on
Victoria Street in 2001, it moved to its
current premises just round the corner in
2011. The shop now sells a daring edit of
contemporary-culture books, magazines
and prints. More than just a store, it is an
excellent place to find inspiration. Owners
Russell Ferguson and Julie Nicoll actively
promote young illustrators and graphic
designers, run occasional talks and
exhibitions, publish a series of art 'zines
and produce limited-edition screen prints
by various local artists.
*39 Candlemaker Row, T 220 0601,
www.analoguebooks.co.uk*

### Anta

For a tartan keepsake, skip the shops flogging cheap tat on the Royal Mile and hit Anta, for everything from porridge bowls to woollen rugs, carpet bags to capsule clothing collections. Here, in the airy flagship store which opened in 2012, you'll swap the bright red, yellow and blue of Royal Stewart for stylish, Farrow & Ball-friendly tones: Highland heather mauve, Glencoe skies grey, and clootie dumpling taupe. Owners Annie and Lachlan Stewart are champions of traditional crafts, and much of their stock is made in Scotland, including the tweed woven in the Borders from yarn sourced from the Western Isles, and the chic oak furniture. If you are able, visit the Highland shop in Fearn (T 01862 832 477) where many items are made.
*119 George Street, T 225 9096,
www.anta.co.uk*

# SPORTS AND SPAS
## WORK OUT, CHILL OUT OR JUST WATCH

Edinburgh is the stepping stone to a host of country pursuits all over Scotland. As a result, the city has some of the best sports accessories shops in the land. Those heading off to hunt can get fully kitted out at Dickson & MacNaughton (21 Frederick Street, T 225 4218). Scotland's rivers attract fishermen from far and wide, and anglers will find all that they need at Gamefish (4 Howe Street, T 220 6465). Golfers who are on their way to St Andrews or the many links courses in East Lothian should visit the Edinburgh Golf Centre (58 Dalry Road, T 337 5888).

Within the city itself, the architecturally acclaimed Dance Base studios (14-16 Grassmarket, T 225 5525) opened in 2001 and has been integral in getting locals moving; the Edinburgh International Climbing Arena (see p092) arrived in the suburbs in 2007; and the Royal Commonwealth Pool (see p068), complete with its new gym, fitness studios and diving pool, has been renovated to Olympic standard. The best pampering option in town is the Sheraton's One Spa (see p090), but The Caledonian (see p024) now offers some competition with the UK's first Guerlain Spa (T 222 8836). Edinburgh's major spectator sports are football and rugby. Football may draw the more partisan crowds, especially when local sides Hibs or Hearts play Glasgow's Rangers or Celtic, but rugby has the far superior stadium in Murrayfield (see p094).

*For full addresses, see Resources.*

## Ruffians

You may arrive hirsute and unkempt, but by the time you've been primped and preened at this concept barbers you'll be every inch the metrosexual. The salon's retro design belies its 21st-century ethos, one that celebrates the barber's ancient art by taking it to another level. The six-step Hot Shave consists of a pampering face scrub, a hot towel, a cut-throat shave, an iced towel, a facial moisturiser and a shoulder, arm and head massage, all using Ruffians' bespoke range of male grooming products. The interior, masterminded by Glasgow-based Graven Images, features dark indigo paintwork, vintage Japanese barbers' chairs, subway tiles and a slick 'waiting room' with a row of iPads as an alternative to crumpled newspapers.
*23 Queensferry Street, T 225 8962, www.ruffians.co.uk*

**One Spa**
Bypass the unsightly Sheraton Grand
Hotel and head for the connecting One
Spa. This luxurious retreat, opened in
2001, offers saunas, steam rooms and a
good range of treatments, but the pièce
de résistance is the mineral-rich rooftop
hydropool (pictured). Open all year, its
temperature is a balmy 33°C to 36°C.
*8 Conference Square, T 221 7777,
www.onespa.com*

## EICA

As the largest indoor climbing facility in the world, the Edinburgh International Climbing Arena (EICA) won a place in the record books for its hometown of Ratho, 20 minutes west of Edinburgh. The state-of-the-art venue is the creation of Edinburgh climbers Rab Anderson and Duncan McCallum, who teamed up with architect David Taylor to create a five-storey structure built into a 30.5m disused quarry. This engineering feat means the centre not only offers 3,000 sq m of artificial climbing, but it is the only indoor complex on the planet that boasts natural rock walls. There is also an aerial rope course, an adventure sports gym, a health club, a café and a lecture theatre, plus various bouldering problems to solve.

*South Platt Hill, Ratho, Newbridge,*
*T 333 6333, www.eica-ratho.com*

### Glenogle Swim Centre

A paean to the Victorian predilection for self-improvement, this is one of several late 19th-century and early 20th-century swimming pools still in operation across the city. Of those that are accessible to the public, council-run Glenogle Baths (as it's known locally) is the most central, sandwiched in-between the Georgian splendour of Saxe-Coburg Place and the quirky B-listed 'colony' houses off Glenogle Road that were built as a philanthropic endeavour. Go for a swim and you can admire the building's architecture from the water. In the lead-up to the site's 2010 refurbishment, local campaigners persuaded the council to keep the glass ceiling, gallery and poolside cubicles that give a dip here so much atmosphere. *Glenogle Road, T 343 6376, www.edinburghleisure.co.uk*

**Murrayfield**

With a capacity of more than 67,000, Murrayfield is one of Britain's largest and most electrifying stadiums. The ground has hosted rugby games since 1925, and the current, structurally expressive bowl was designed by Connor Milligan Architects and completed in 1994. The impressive arena comes into its own for international fixtures, such as Six Nations ties, for which tickets are like gold dust. In addition to rugby union, American football and The Highland Games have been played here, as, occasionally, have rugby league and football matches. It has even hosted a youth rally to welcome the Pope, and is a popular venue for music concerts. Behind-the-scenes tours take in the pitch, dressing rooms and hospitality suites. *Roseburn Street, T 346 5160, www.scottishrugby.org*

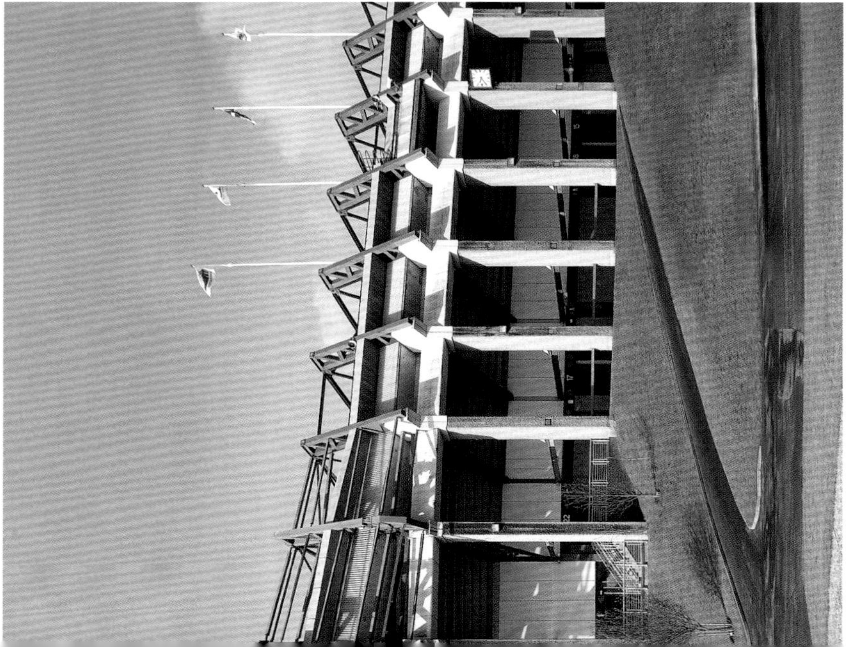

# ESCAPES

## WHERE TO GO IF YOU WANT TO LEAVE TOWN

Edinburgh's modest size means that getting out is quick and easy. A short taxi ride can transport you to dramatic scenery, while further afield, by car or train, are breathtaking surroundings and myriad outdoor activities, especially around Peebles to the south.

Musselburgh is a quaint seaside fishing town that is convenient for a day trip. Less contaminated by amusement arcades and chip shops than its larger neighbour Portobello, it is home to one of the best gelaterias in Europe, S Luca (32-38 High Street, T 665 2237), open for business since 1908 and alone worth the six-mile journey.

Self-catering properties are a perfect way to explore Scotland's hills, beaches and lochs. Chic options abound: in the far north-west are the contemporary Hill Croft and Shore Croft (bookable via www.croft103.com), while craft and design retailer Papa Stour (www.papastour.com) refurbished the rustic Callakille cottage (Applecross, T 01456 486 358). In the western Highlands, some 40 minutes by train from Fort William, the Corrour country estate (www.corrour.co.uk) features several cottages, some decorated by Suzy Hoodless. But the Isle of Skye has the most impressive selection, numbering 15 Fiskavaig (see p100) and the Timber House (www.timberhouse-skye.co.uk) among its many hideaways. The highly regarded Three Chimneys restaurant with rooms (Colbost, T 01470 511 258) is a key part of the island's appeal.

*For full addresses, see Resources.*

### Jupiter Artland, Wilkieston

Open from mid-May until mid-September, this art gallery and sculpture park, half an hour from Edinburgh by car, launched in 2009. Commissioning many of the major names in contemporary art to make work in situ in one reasonably compact space, co-owner Nicky Wilson has proved what can be done with a touch of vision – and some private investment. Fans of Charles Jencks' *Landform* at the Scottish National Gallery of Modern Art (T 624 6200), can here admire his dramatic installation *Cells of Life* (overleaf), a series of vast, swirling earthwork knolls. It forms a mighty full-stop to a tour of large-scale pieces by Andy Goldsworthy, Antony Gormley, Cornelia Parker and others, which have included Jim Lambie's *ZOBOP (Fluorescent)* (above). *Bonnington House Steadings, T 01506 889 900, www.jupiterartland.org*

### 15 Fiscavaig, Isle of Skye

Dubbed the Hen House, this modern two-bedroom timber-clad retreat on Skye's Minginish Peninsula was the work of Rural Design Architects, and the project claimed the Saltire Medal in 2010, a year after completion. The home rises out of the raw landscape, lifted off the uneven ground on small piloti; the two-storey southern end of the building slopes down to a single level on the northern tip, which leans into the winds. Inside it's airy, open-plan and, crucially, warm, thanks to thick insulation and a wood-burning stove. Floor-to-ceiling windows frame great views of the coast. Fiscavaig beach is within walking distance, and the brooding Cuillins are nearby for Munro-baggers. Inverness is the closest airport, a three-hour drive away.
*Fiscavaig, T 07891 199 569,*
*www.15fiscavaig.co.uk*

**The Falkirk Wheel**
This engineering solution connecting the Forth and Clyde Canal with the Union Canal has not only restored navigability across Scotland, but the *Return of the Jedi*-like structure has also become a slightly offbeat tourist attraction. Opened in 2002, the world's first rotating boat lift replaces the former, tedious system of 11 locks. Boats entering the upper gondola are lowered, along with the water they float in, to the basin below. At the same time, an equal weight is lifted in the lower gondola. Don't get it? Take a trip yourself, starting at the Visitor Centre. Boats are first gracefully lifted by the gondola 35m up to the Union Canal and then sail through the Rough Castle Tunnel, under the historic Antonine Wall, before returning to the Wheel to be rotated down again.
*Lime Road, Tamfourhill, Falkirk, T 08700 500 208, www.thefalkirkwheel.co.uk*

# NOTES

**SKETCHES AND MEMOS**

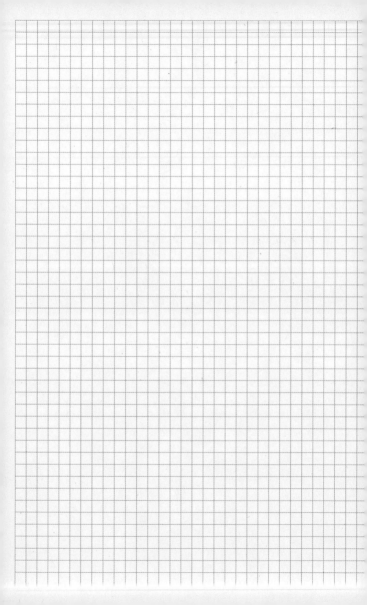

# RESOURCES
## CITY GUIDE DIRECTORY

**A**

**Analogue** 085
*39 Candlemaker Row*
*T 220 0601*
*www.analoguebooks.co.uk*

**Anta** 086
*119 George Street*
*T 225 9096*
*Fearn*
*Tain*
*Ross-shire*
*T 01862 832 477*
*www.anta.co.uk*

**Armstrongs** 080
*83 Grassmarket*
*T 220 5557*
*www.armstrongsvintage.co.uk*

**Artisan Roast** 062
*57 Broughton Street*
*T 07526 236 615*
*www.artisanroast.co.uk*

**B**

**Bia Bistrot** 052
*19 Colinton Road*
*T 452 8453*
*www.biabistrot.co.uk*

**Bramble** 044
*16a Queen Street*
*T 226 6343*
*www.bramblebar.co.uk*

**Bruichladdich** 081
*Isle of Islay*
*T 01496 850 190*
*www.bruichladdich.com*

**C**

**Castle Terrace** 040
*33-35 Castle Terrace*
*T 229 1222*
*www.castleterracerestaurant.com*

**Catalog Ltd** 080
*2-4 St Stephen Place*
*T 225 2888*
*www.cataloginteriors.com*

**Concrete Wardrobe** 080
*50a Broughton Street*
*T 558 7130*

**Crombies** 062
*97-101 Broughton Street*
*T 557 0111*
*www.sausages.co.uk*

**D**

**Dance Base** 088
*14-16 Grassmarket*
*T 225 5525*
*www.dancebase.co.uk*

**Dick's** 062
*3 North West Circus Place*
*T 226 6220*
*www.dicks-edinburgh.co.uk*

**Dickson & MacNaughton** 088
*21 Frederick Street*
*T 225 4218*
*www.dicksonandmacnaughton.com*

**The Dogs** 036
*110 Hanover Street*
*T 220 1208*
*www.thedogsonline.co.uk*

**Dovecot Café by Stag Espresso** 076
*Dovecot Studios*
*10 Infirmary Street*
*T 07590 728 974*
*www.stagespresso.com*

# HOTELS

## ADDRESSES AND ROOM RATES

**The Atholl** 018
Room rates:
Suite, from £1,000;
The Abercromby, £2,500
*11 Atholl Crescent*
*T 08447 360 047*
*www.theatholl.com*

**The Balmoral** 016
Room rates:
double, from £180
*1 Princes Street*
*T 556 2414*
*www.thebalmoralhotel.com*

**The Caledonian** 024
Room rates:
double, from £140
*Princes Street*
*T 222 8890*
*www.thecaledonianedinburgh.com*

**Callakille** 096
Room rates:
double, from £465
*Applecross*
*Wester Ross*
*T 01456 486 358*
*www.wildernesscottages.co.uk*

**Corrour** 096
Room rates:
Cottage, from £300 per week
*Inverness-Shire*
*T 01397 732 200*
*www.corrour.co.uk*

**15 Fiscavaig** 100
Room rates:
House, from £500 per week
*Fiscavaig*
*Isle of Skye*
*T 07891 199 569*
*www.15fiscavaig.co.uk*

**The Glasshouse** 016
Room rates:
double, from £125
*2 Greenside Place*
*T 525 8200*
*www.theglasshousehotel.co.uk*

**Hill Croft** 096
Room rates:
House, from £1,400 per week
*Loch Eriboll*
*Sutherland*
*T 01971 511 202*
*www.croft103.com*

**The Howard** 029
Room rates:
double, from £150;
Abercromby Suite, £315
*34 Great King Street*
*T 557 3500*
*www.thehoward.com*

**Hotel Missoni** 022
Room rates:
double, from £205;
Room 507, £225;
Suite D'Argento, £900
*1 George IV Bridge*
*T 220 6666*
*www.hotelmissoni.com*

**Motel One** 016
Room rates:
double, from £70
*18-21 Market Street*
*T 220 0730*
*www.motel-one.com*

**94DR** 020
Room rates:
double, from £100;
The Bowmore, £150
*94 Dalkeith Road*
*T 662 9265*
*www.94dr.com*

**One Royal Circus** 028
Room rates:
double, from £70;
Suites, from £90
*1 Royal Circus*
*T 625 6669*
*www.oneroyalcircus.com*

**Prestonfield** 026
Room rates:
double, from £295;
Allan Ramsay Suite, from £360
*Priestfield Road*
*T 225 7800*
*www.prestonfield.com*

**Shore Croft** 096
Room rates:
House, from £1,400 per week
*Loch Eriboll*
*Sutherland*
*T 01971 511 202*
*www.croft103.com*

**The Three Chimneys** 096
Room rates:
double, from £295
*Colbost*
*Dunvegan*
*Isle of Skye*
*T 01470 511 258*
*www.threechimneys.co.uk*

**Tigerlily** 030
Room rates:
double, £230;
Georgian Suite, from £430
*125 George Street*
*T 225 5005*
*www.tigerlilyedinburgh.co.uk*

**Timber House** 096
Room rates:
House, from £500 per week
*Skinidin*
*Isle of Skye*
*T 557 4800*
*www.timberhouse-skye.co.uk*

**The Witchery** 017
Room rates:
Suite, from £295;
Old Rectory, from £295;
Heriot Suite, from £295
*Castlehill*
*The Royal Mile*
*T 225 5613*
*www.thewitchery.com*

## WALLPAPER* CITY GUIDES

**Executive Editor**
Rachael Moloney

**Editor**
Ella Marshall
**Authors**
Rhiannon Batten
Lucy Gilmore

**Art Director**
Loran Stosskopf
**Art Editor**
Eriko Shimazaki
**Designer**
Mayumi Hashimoto
**Map Illustrator**
Russell Bell

**Photography Editor**
Elisa Merlo
**Assistant Photography Editor**
Nabil Butt

**Chief Sub-Editor**
Nick Mee
**Sub-Editor**
Farah Shafiq

**Editorial Assistant**
Emma Harrison

**Interns**
Hugo Arthur Raymond
Maja Šćepanović
Romy van den Broeke

**Wallpaper* Group Editor-in-Chief**
Tony Chambers
**Publishing Director**
Gord Ray
**Managing Editor**
Oliver Adamson

**Contributor**
Alex Bagner

Wallpaper* ® is a registered trademark of IPC Media Limited

First published 2008
Revised and updated 2012 and 2013

All prices are correct at the time of going to press, but are subject to change.

Printed in China

## PHAIDON

**Phaidon Press Limited**
Regent's Wharf
All Saints Street
London N1 9PA

**Phaidon Press Inc**
180 Varick Street
New York, NY 10014

Phaidon® is a registered trademark of Phaidon Press Limited

www.phaidon.com

A CIP Catalogue record for this book is available from the British Library.

ISBN 978 0 7148 6620 8

# PHOTOGRAPHERS

**Benjamin Blossom**
Edinburgh Castle,
pp010-011
McEwan Hall, p012
National Monument, p013
One Royal Circus, p028
The Howard, p029
Tigerlily, pp030-031
Urban Angel, p033
Kay's Bar, p045
Peter's Yard, p053
The Shore Bar &
Restaurant, p057
Sweet Melindas,
pp060-061
National Museum of
Scotland, p065,
pp066-067
Royal Commonwealth
Pool, pp068-069
Scottish Parliament,
pp070-071
Old College, p072
Scottish Storytelling
Centre, p073
Randolph Crescent,
pp074-075
One Spa, pp090-091
Murrayfield, pp094-095

**Canestraro &
Di Pasquale**
Forth Rail
Bridge, pp014-015
The Witchery, p017
The Atholl, p018, p019
Scottish National Portrait
Gallery, p034, p035
The Gardener's
Cottage, p039
Restaurant Mark
Greenaway, p041
Earthy, pp042-043
Kanpai, p046, p047
Timberyard, pp048-049
Sheep Heid
Inn, pp054-055
Fee and
Adam Storey, p063
Walker Slater, pp082-083
Life Story, p084
Anta, p086, p087
Ruffians, p089
Edinburgh International
Climbing Arena, p092

**Matt Clayton**
94DR, pp020-021
Hotel Missoni, p022, p023
Prestonfield, p026, p027
Bramble, p044
21212, pp050-051

Bia Bistrot, p052
Ondine, p056
Dovecot Studios,
pp076-077
Royal Botanic
Garden, pp078-079
Analogue, p085
Glenogle Swim
Centre, p093

**Jerry Driendl/
Getty Images**
Edinburgh city view,
inside front cover

**Andrew Lee**
15 Fiscavaig, p100, p101

**John McKenzie**
Ingleby Gallery, p038

**Peartree Digital**
Bruichladdich The Organic
2010 whisky, p081

**Allan Pollok-Morris**
Jupiter Artland, p097,
pp098-099

# EDINBURGH

## A COLOUR-CODED GUIDE TO THE HOT 'HOODS

### LEITH
Once a gritty port in north-east Edinburgh, the waterfront is now sought-after real estate

### SOUTHSIDE/NEWINGTON
This sprawling borough is characterised by green spaces, academic buildings and theatres

### NEW TOWN
A feast of Georgian architecture, James Craig's urban idyll is city planning at its finest

### OLD TOWN
Sidestep the tourist traps to marvel at the medieval splendour of this World Heritage Site

### WEST END/TOLLCROSS/BRUNTSFIELD
Gentrifying fast, these zones are now home to the middle classes, chichi stores and delis

### CANONGATE
Numerous historic and modern landmarks are packed into this small corner of the city

For a full description of each neighbourhood, see the Introduction.
Featured venues are colour-coded, according to the district in which they are located.